Mickey Maloney

Written by Jill Eggleton
Illustrated by Trevor Pye

Mickey Maloney was a spy.
He went spying at night
with his spy bag.
He had a list of
spying jobs to do.

Jobs For Mickey Maloney

1) Go to Number 3 Cook Street
   and find out who is eating
   the cat's dinner.

2) Go to Number 10 Green Street
   and find out who is eating
   the apples off the tree.

3) Go to Number 8 Dunk Street
   and find out who is making
   holes in the garden.

Mickey Maloney ran across
Mrs Morrow's garden.
He made big footprints
with his spy shoes,
but it was dark
and he didn't see.

He went to
Number 3 Cook Street.
He looked over the fence
and he saw a hedgehog
eating the cat's dinner.

He went to
Number 10 Green Street
and he saw snails
eating the apples.

He went to
Number 8 Dunk Street
and he saw big worms
making holes in the garden.

Mickey Maloney crossed off
all the things on his list.

Jobs For Mickey Maloney

1) Go to Number 3 Cook Street
   and find out who is eating
   the cat's dinner.

2) Go to Number 10 Green Street
   and find out who is eating
   the apples off the tree.

3) Go to Number 8 Dark Street
   and find out who is making
   holes in the garden.

Then he went home
to sleep.

But Mrs Morrow
was not asleep.
She saw someone in a black
hat and black glasses go into
Mickey Maloney's house!
Mrs Morrow called the police.
"Come quickly!" she said.
"A robber is going
into Mickey Maloney's house!"

11

The police came and knocked
on Mickey Maloney's door.
"Is there a robber
in your house?" they said.

"No," said Mickey Maloney.
"There is just me."

The police saw Mickey
Maloney's spy pyjamas.
They saw a spy bag.
"You are a spy," they said.
And they laughed.

Internet

Top Secret:
Use code **S**
to decode message:
Yellow bananas
at Dot's place.

The next day, Mickey Maloney
gave Mrs Morrow a card.

Mickey Maloney - Spy
Phone : 2743761
Fax : 2745481
E.mail: mickeymaloney@dakata.com

"You are a spy,"
said Mrs Morrow.
"Good! Find out who made
the footprints in my garden!"

A List

Clothes

glasses

coat

wig

boots

hat

gloves

Gear

binoculars

rope

torch

bag

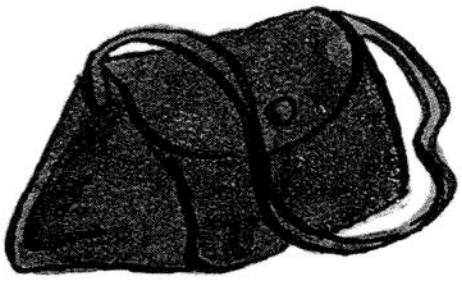

watch

magnifying glass

Guide Notes

Title: **Mickey Maloney**

Stage: Early (4) – Green

Genre: Fiction

Approach: Guided Reading

Processes: Thinking Critically, Exploring Language, Processing Information

Written and Visual Focus: Lists

Word Count: 290

THINKING CRITICALLY

(sample questions)
- What do you think this story could be about?
- Look at the cover. Who do you think this person could be?
- Look at pages 2 and 3. Why do you think Mickey Maloney is dressed like that? Why do you think he needs sunglasses at night?
- Look at page 4. What do you notice Mickey Maloney is leaving in the garden?
- Why do you think Mickey Maloney goes spying at night?
- Look at pages 10 and 11. What do you think Mrs Morrow is going to do?
- Look at pages 12 and 13. How can you tell Mickey Maloney's house belongs to a spy?

EXPLORING LANGUAGE

Terminology
Title, cover, illustrations, author, illustrator

Vocabulary
Interest words: spy, magnifying glass
High-frequency word: things
Positional words: off, in, across, over, into, on
Compound words: footprints, hedgehog, asleep, someone, into, across

Print Conventions
Capital letter for sentence beginnings, titles, names (Mickey Maloney, Mrs Morrow) and place names (Cook Street, Green Street, Dunk Street), full stops, exclamation marks, quotation marks, commas, question mark